Once A Rotarian, Always A Rotarian

Sean M. Teaford

authorHOUSE®

AuthorHouse™
1663 Liberty Drive
Bloomington, IN 47403
www.authorhouse.com
Phone: 1 (800) 839-8640

Published by AuthorHouse   04/25/2016

ISBN: 978-1-5049-8625-0 (sc)
ISBN: 978-1-5049-8686-1 (e)

Library of Congress Control Number: 2016904753

Print information available on the last page.

This book is printed on acid-free paper.

Dedicated to all Rotarians, past and present, who exemplify the motto "Service Above Self"

Acknowledgements

_____

This book would not be possible without the kindness, support, and generosity shown to me over the years by the members of the Rotary Club of Bala Cynwyd – Narberth, Rotary District 7450, and all the great Rotarians whom I have had the pleasure to meet. In particular, I would like to give special thanks to Rotarian Richard M. Trivane who immediately welcomed me into Rotary, guided me during my time as an active member, supported me in my Rotary endeavors, and has aided me in maintaining my connection to the club.

Of course, the one person who needs to be thanked more than anyone else is my wife who has allowed me to dedicate so much time to Rotary and many other service and fraternal organizations throughout the year.

Lastly, I would like to thank those who have assisted me at Author House (especially Joseph Elas), my fellow Rotarians, family, friends, followers, and occasional readers of my blog, Time To Keep It Simple, where these short essays were first published as well as the many Rotary districts around the world who included some of these essays in their newsletters.

Contents

Is it the TRUTH?

An Introduction About My Rotary Journey

Is it FAIR to all concerned?

A Fair And Balanced Forum For All Guest Speakers!

Does it promote GOOD WILL and BETTER FRIENDSHIP?

Offering Guidance And Assistance To ALL Rotarians

Will it be BENEFICIAL to all concerned?

Important Takeaways From RLI And Other Rotary Events

Other Works By Sean M. Teaford

———

Teaching A Stone To Talk: Nature Poems (Bending Tree Press, 2003)

Kaddish Diary (Pudding House Publications, 2005)

Paintings In Under A Thousand Words: Nature Poems (Author House, 2016)

What Was Not Said: Echoes From The Holocaust (Author House, 2016)

Out On The Limbs: Searching For Answers In The Family Tree (Author House, 2016)

The Good, The Bad, And The Adorable: My First Year As A Father (Author House, 2016)

Is it the TRUTH?

An Introduction About My Rotary Journey

Rotary Filled The Void

———

When my wife and I moved back to the Philadelphia area we were put in a situation where there was a huge amount of uncertainty. While we were close to both of our families, which was the impetus for the move back from Israel, we were in a new town, unemployed, and trying to figure out what we were going to do. With both of us having found some form of employment in the first half of 2012, we were still trying to find ways to become a part of the community rather than simply a couple that rented an apartment in the area.

While my wife found her own way and started volunteering with the Philly Friendship Circle (I joined her on several occasions), it wasn't until later that summer when I found my way of joining the community. After attending a few meetings during the summer, I was inducted into the Rotary Club of Bala Cynwyd – Narberth in August and was immediately given the opportunity to not just attend but be an active participant in the club. I was honored and appreciative of the trust put in me and the investment that all the members made in helping me develop not just as a leader but as a human being.

Over the next year there remained many uncertainties in my life with only a few substantial exceptions one of which was Rotary. Every week I knew I could rely on Rotary to both ground me and inspire me to do better, work harder, and embrace all that life has to offer. Rotary filled a void during that year, an empty space that I didn't realize existed long before the uncertainty descended upon me.

The essays that follow were originally written as posts for my blog, Time To Keep It Simple, which has long since served as a daily record of my life as a traveler, writer, genealogist, photographer, Rotarian, Mason, Jew, PR professional, and many other (mostly positive) things. However, those original posts have been divided into sections according to The Four Way Test which is recited before every Rotary meeting and serves as a means to guide the actions of every Rotarian. The questions we ask ourselves every day are as follows:

- Is it the TRUTH?
- Is it FAIR to all concerned?
- Does it promote GOOD WILL and BETTER FRIENDSHIP?
- Will it be BENEFICIAL to all concerned?

While my activity within Rotary has been limited in recent years, the lessons that I learned while an active member of my club continue to influence my life. The friendships formed during that time are some of my most treasured and I will forever be thankful for the support that I continue to receive from my fellow Rotarians. However, most importantly, my time as a Rotarian has given me the skills and passion for service and community that has made me a better leader, person, husband, and father.

Schedule Shift

———

This week I missed my Rotary meeting for the first time in months. There have been a few close calls from time to time but I outright missed it yesterday. This is not a unique problem. Many Rotarians have to adjust their schedules to find the time to attend a meeting. It is the commitment we made when we joined Rotary. Sometimes things work out and you can find a way to attend your home club meeting. But that is not always the case.

Given my new daily routine, I am going to have to find a number of clubs to fit into my calendar. I will do my best to occasionally attend meetings at my home club in Bala Cynwyd but, at this point, I can't guarantee anything. It will continue to be my home club but most of my meetings will have to be beyond the confines of Aldar Bistro.

What does that mean for some of the projects I have undertaken? Nothing, I am still going to work as hard as I have been on them. This schedule shift may even be to my benefit as it will give my club, our projects, and our raffle greater exposure.

What I will miss are the people. These people are not just my fellow Rotarians or club members; they are my friends who have been there for me during much of this recent rough patch. They will always be dear friends and I will continue to talk to and coordinate with them regarding the goings on in the club and what they happen to be doing beyond the Rotary world.

You may not see as many posts regarding the speakers at my club, which should have been obvious by now. But I will write about all the events, conferences, training programs and visitations to other clubs that I experience moving forward. In fact, you will be (or maybe you won't if you tend to skip over these posts) reading about a Rotary event that I will be attending on Saturday when I finally finish up with Rotary Leadership Institute (RLI).

So, some things are definitely going to change in my own Rotary world but many things are going to stay the same. Change is good most of the time and in this instance it has the potential to be great. Stay tuned for a different Rotary perspective.

Rotary Letter

––––

The last few months have been hectic but that is nothing new to those who have been following this blog. What I haven't really written about at length is my ongoing dilemma with regard to Rotary. While I have touched upon the scheduling difficulties from time to time I haven't spoken of the back and forth in my own mind regarding my continued participation with my club. Although sometimes there is a lot of information to be found in the unsaid as Rotary posts have been lacking for some time now.

Not long ago I received a message on my cell phone from a fellow Rotarian from my club and the immediate past President. It caught me a little off guard as I had not let my thoughts go that far… his message was asking whether or not I was going to resign from the club and if I was going to do so I would have to submit a letter of notification by the middle of the month. It was a wrenching thought to consider but it was a reality that I knew I had to face. After many days, this is the letter I have written with my final, albeit temporary, decision:

Dear BCN Club President,

It is with great sadness that I write this letter. At this time, I must resign both as an officer and as a member of the Rotary Club of Bala Cynwyd – Narberth.

Due to my increasing number of commitments on my schedule combined with my extended work day, I am unable to attend the prerequisite number of meetings in order to sustain my membership in the club or in Rotary. This is the sole reason for my resignation. It is simply a matter of timing.

Moving forward, if the club would be willing to accept, I would like to continue my affiliation with the club as a "Friend of Rotary". If there are other options available, please let me now but, to the best of my knowledge, this is the only option available with regard to retaining a connection with the club.

As you know, Rotary is an amazing organization to be a part of and I cherish every moment and memory that I have of the club, the district, and Rotary International as a whole. I look forward to continuing my Rotary service in the future when I will be able to set aside the time and effort that I feel is necessary.

Moving forward, I hope to continue our friendship and I hope to make the occasional appearance at Aldar Bistro as well as other Rotary events.

Please call or email me with any questions or concerns.

Thank you and please thank everyone at the BCN Club for all the help, support, and encouragement during my time in Rotary.

Yours In Rotary Service,

Sean

Time is something that will always be a limited quantity and I will never have enough to do all the things that I want to do. That being the reality, sometimes things just don't make sense when you have to keep a schedule. I try to fit as many activities, groups, and events in my calendar and Rotary just doesn't seem to fit at this specific point in my life. Will I return to Rotary? That is the plan and I hope that it will be sooner rather than later. Keep in mind that I will continue to participate whenever and where ever I am able but the weekly meetings are an unrealistic option. For now I say good bye quickly followed with see you soon.

Thinking Back There Seems
To Be Something Missing

―――――

Every week I am amazed at how fast time seems to be drifting by. Every once in a while I stop for a moment, look back, and think about all that I have been able to do, see, and accomplish. However, this time around, I noticed something missing from my memories.

Truth be told, I haven't been able to attend a Rotary meeting since September or October and while I have done my best to keep up to date with everything going on (thanks in large part to the weekly phone messages from my club) there is still a gap in my memory. Obviously, there is a huge difference between experiencing something and simply hearing about it. And because I really only write about my thoughts and experiences, there has been a lack of Rotary related posts since the last time I was surrounded by my fellow Rotarians.

That is something else that I struggle with. While I am still an Honorary Rotarian, I am pretty far removed at this point from the goings on in my club and in my district. Personally, I don't know if I should really be called a Rotarian. Don't get me wrong, I take great pride in my affiliation, but I really can't say that I am earning that honor at this point. That is how I honestly feel at this point. With that said, I still carry the Four Way Test with me as a reminder and I still have a plethora of pins that are used in a Rotary rotation but that has been about the limit of my connection over the past half year.

I'm not sure if my current situation is fair to my club and to all the great people that I have had the pleasure of getting to know since I originally became a member in August 2012. I consider them all great friends who have supported me during a difficult transition period in my career but, since getting things back on track, I have not been able to enjoy their company. However, that only accounts for the meetings. I have not kept in touch with the club as I should have been doing all along. For that, I really don't have a reason or an excuse.

It just goes to show that for many of us if we are not present and active in a club, organization, or fraternity we gradually become a bit disconnected both from the entity and from the people. I saw everyone once a week for over a year and now I haven't seen them for over 6 months. A group of people and an organization that was once a large part of my recollection and reflection is now oddly absent. I think it is time to change that. At the very least, I should pick up the phone.

Returning To Rotary... For A Night

Ever since I began working 'normal' hours I haven't been able to make it to a Rotary meeting especially at my home club which meets for lunch in the middle of the week. Logistically it just hasn't worked out. Of course, there have been other activities that have kept me occupied but I have only been able to schedule so much before my wife gets that look in her eyes. And, honestly, I can't say I blame her. There is only so much I can do without burning out and I have to have time at home or else I will just start shutting down.

However, last night, for the first time in months, I was able to once again join my fellow Rotarians in Bala Cynwyd for a wonderful dinner and, as always, excellent discussion. On what would have been my induction night as President of the club, I sat at one of the four crowded tables in the back room of Aldar Bistro and watched as another Rotarian took office. It was interesting to think about what could have been but that moment was fleeting because, while I may not be involved in Rotary like I once was, there are a lot of other things that I enjoy in what I consider to be a great life.

Unexpectedly, the new president gave a bit of a hat tip to me as in the short time I was active in Rotary and at the club, I made what turned out to be a positive impact. As I have said before, sometimes work and life in general can get in the way of things like Rotary but what is really important is that we remain active in our desire to give back and do good work. After all, we each have the responsibility to bring light to the world because while one candle may only be able to make a pin point in the dark, if we each hold a candle we can turn night into day. Rotary is just one of the many places where you can old your candle high.

By the end of the evening there were many people I had caught up with, many to whom I was introduced, and most that I had a chance to talk with about the long time that had passed. While I doubt that there will be time in the near future when I will be able to attend another meeting, I look forward to the next gathering I will be able to attend and I am determined to do a better job in keeping the line of communication open with my old club. Regardless of what happens, I will never forget what my club and Rotary did for me during a difficult period, the welcoming receptions that I continue to receive whenever I am able to make it to a meeting, gathering, or event, and what it continues to do as it influences my daily life.

Back To Rotary: Upcoming Presentations

———

When I felt my phone vibrate I immediately thought it was one of the usual family or lodge suspects sending me an update or asking me a question. What I didn't expect to read when I opened up my text messages was a request from the President of the Rotary Club of Bala Cynwyd – Narberth to be a guest speaker at one of the upcoming meetings. While it has been some time since I was last a regular member, I am still proud to hold the title of Honorary Rotarian and it will certainly be a privilege and pleasure to reconnect with the people who have continued to support me despite my long absence. Following our brief conversation, I will not only have one opportunity to revisit this find group but two opportunities to join them for lunch in the coming months.

The first presentation I will be making is on the transforming my everyday experiences into a daily blog and, recently, into a collection of books. I started my blog while still very active with the club and I have continued writing daily posts. Now numbering over a thousand, I have begun the process of transforming those posts into essay collections on individual topics.

The first book to result from this effort is *The Good, The Bad, And The Adorable: My First Year As A Father* which recounts all the moments from the time my wife and I found out we were having a baby all the way through my son's first birthday. I guess you could call it a baby book on steroids. The second book, *Out On the Limbs: Searching For Answers In The Family Tree*, was released at the same time and includes many of the family stories that have been passed down to me as well as the recreations of some of the lives of my ancestors which I have pieced together through years of research. Of course, there are numerous more on the way this year but this gives you a sense of the subject of this presentation.

While genealogy is a topic that I have discussed before during a meeting this presentation will be completely different than the last one. The second presentation, which was actually the original impetus for the outreach, will be on the research, application process, and joining the Sons of the American Revolution. This has been a goal for several years and now it is finally coming to fruition. During this presentation I will not only talk about the discovery of this family line which was unfamiliar to the family during my youth but the process of researching and ultimately proving this lineage to the point where it will stand up to the scrutiny of an independent third party such as the Sons of the American Revolution. Of course, this is just the beginning and I will also touch upon the repetition of this process that is before me as I begin pulling together the documentation for thirty supplemental applications.

All that is left is to coordinate a day that works in my schedule. Hopefully, this will be a regular commitment as I continue writing and researching… there are certainly enough topics that I can speak on, maybe not intelligently but enough for a presentation. But, for now, I will enjoy the opportunity to visit my club, share my passions, and spend a couple of days with some great friends.

Is it FAIR to all concerned?

A Fair And Balanced Forum For All Guest Speakers!

The Pressing Educational Needs Of The Community

As some of you may know I am currently serving as the Sergeant-at-Arms for The Rotary Club of Bala Cynwyd – Narberth. This post is the first in a series regarding the diverse presentations made at my local Rotary club. Occasionally, I will also write posts about the club that I happen to be visiting as well as any events or training that I attend.

The Rotary Club of Bala Cynwyd - Narberth was honored to have Rotarian John Bannan, Founder and Executive Director of the Philadelphia Children's Foundation and member of The Rotary Club of Northeast Sunrisers in Philadelphia, as there guest speaker during their weekly meeting on Wednesday, November 21st, 2012 at Aldar Bistro in Bala Cynwyd, Pennsylvania. Mr. Bannan delivered a compelling and educational talk regarding the pressing needs of Philadelphia's youth and the staggering statistics that plague the city's public school system. Some of those stunning figures are as follows:

- Over 50% of ninth graders in the Philadelphia public schools between 2000 and 2005 did not graduate in four years.
- In any one year, about 8,000 students officially dropped out and an additional 5,000 spent so little time in school that researchers called them dropouts.
- Only 78.5% of Philadelphia's 25+ year old population graduated high school.
- The Philadelphia SD ranks only 65th in overall graduation rates among the 100 largest school districts in the country.
- Over 90,000 students and families in the Philadelphia School District don't have a computer at home.

"Those statistics, among others, are what motivated me to form the Philadelphia Children's Foundation," said Bannan. "The future of our city hinges on the education of our children and I will continue to dedicate myself to improving our future."

The foundation is not only providing education but direction for many school age kids by facilitating the donation and distribution of computers and books while also arranging for guest speakers, mentors, and internships.

"The work being achieved through the Philadelphia Children's Foundation is impressive in both its scope and its impact," commented Rick Trivane, President of The Rotary Club of Bala Cynwyd - Narberth. "John epitomizes the Rotary motto of "service above self" and we can all learn a great deal by following his example."

The Philadelphia Children's Foundation is always looking for people to donate their books, computers, and/or time. Together we can bring about change that can last for generations.

Overcoming Able Bodied Bias

———

This week we welcomed Michael Kelly who serves as volunteer coordinator at the Inglis House in Philadelphia. Our club has a long standing relationship with Inglis and we are proud of the partnership which has continuously strengthened over the years. With that said, we greatly appreciated Michael taking the time to reintroduce us to the services that Inglis provides to those in need and the inspiration that their programs provide to both participants and the community in general.

Founded in 1877, Inglis House is a specialty nursing care facility providing long-term, residential care for 297 adults with physical disabilities, including multiple sclerosis, cerebral palsy, spinal cord injury and stroke, among others. Residents receive rehabilitative medical and nursing care; physical, occupational and speech therapies; and a selection of more than 20 social enrichment and therapeutic recreation programs every day.

Inglis Community Based Services supports more than 800 people living independently in the community through resources including: accessible housing, care management (helping people navigate the health care system), a day program, an MS Evening program and community employment. Inglis is also the largest provider of affordable accessible housing in the Greater Philadelphia region with 208 housing units, and plans for 50 more units by 2015.

All Inglis services and programs are designed to enable people with physical disabilities to enjoy life with the greatest amount of independence and mobility.

It is important to note that Inglis provides services for people from all walks of life and with a wide variety and degree of disabilities all the while emphasizing and encouraging the amazing talents and abilities locked inside uncooperative bodies that are sometimes overlooked by the community.

I encourage you to consider donating your time, either on your own or through an organization such as Rotary, by assisting these amazing individuals in expressing the intelligence and passion that lies just beneath the surface. It will certainly change your perspective and make you appreciate the simple tasks that many of us take for granted. It might also lead you to question your own misconceptions and sever the connection between intelligence and physical ability.

From Venezuela to the US to South Korea

———

This week we had a great opportunity to start off the new Rotary year with a great speaker, Ruben Reyes, who was sponsored by The Rotary Club of Northeast Sunrisers in Philadelphia to be a part of The Rotary District 7450 Group Study Exchange Experience in Seoul, South Korea this past April. As part of a five person exchange, Mr. Reyes spent four weeks abroad learning about Korean culture and cultivating good will as one of the representatives from our Rotary district. Our club also had the opportunity to meet the Korean team during their visit in April to the Philadelphia area.

A native of Venezuela, Mr. Reyes resides in Philadelphia and is a Principal and Founding Partner of Lyquix, a marketing and technology firm based in Philadelphia, responsible for overseeing all the technology and usability aspects of projects. Given his marketing and technology background, he offered an interesting perspective of both the experience and the progress that surrounded the team throughout the exchange. Other members of the team comprised of other nationalities and professions which provided for a dynamic and interesting experience for all.

"Being part of the GSE team is at the same time an honor, and a very exciting adventure. As I was expecting, our team represents very diverse professions, aptitudes, and personalities. What I didn't expect was to find that 3 out of 5 of us are born and raised outside the US. Blandine is from France, Tae is from Thailand, and I am from Venezuela." Mr. Reyes continued, "While, we certainly don't represent the struggles of immigrants that have escaped oppression, war, or poverty, for whom freedom and prosperity was denied to them in their home lands, we are proud to have the opportunity to visit South Korea to promote goodwill from both the U.S. and our home countries. This team truly represents the notion that the United States is a melting pot of cultures."

All present at the weekly meeting were impressed with the way Mr. Reyes presented himself and how the members of the GSE team represented the district. We were also intrigued to find out about some of the many cultural and Rotary related differences between our two countries most notably the sheer volume of food present at meals and the fact that certain Rotary clubs have their own buildings. Overall, the message presented to the club reinforced our previous experience from our international guests from District 3600 months ago that the people of South Korea are incredibly warm, good hearted, and motivated by a love of peace and community.

The GSE program is something that we are all looking forward to hearing about again from both sides in the future as it illustrates one of the beauties of being a part of the world's largest service centric organization. The connection we all share as Rotarians goes beyond language, culture, and country. Service knows no boundaries and peace needs no translation.

To read more about The Rotary District 7450 Group Study Exchange Experience in Seoul, South Korea this past April visit the team's blog athttp://phillygse2013.wordpress.com/.

Presenting Members With Alternatives

———

Time and again I read about proponents making grandiose claims about alternative medicine whether it is a miracle pill/supplement, a bracelet that can cure you from pain, or a drastic diet that can turn you into an Adonis. Every time I find myself changing the channel, turning the page, or leaving the room. But there are other times when I sit back, listen, and once they are done preaching I ask them a very simple question. I never ask anything tricky or that is an attempt to catch them in a trap. Every time I have done this my question has been either dismissed or I am given a general claim that their snake oil can cure anything.

Given my past experiences, I went into the Rotary meeting with some underlying consternation but, to be fair, I sat back and I listened. Our guest speaker's background was so diversified that I couldn't help but give her my attention and see what her view is on her chosen profession. It was also in the best interest of the club that I remain neutral as I was acting President yesterday and I didn't want to interfere or have a negative impact on the club.

After opening the meeting in both the traditional and in our own unique manner, I was honored to be a part of a long overdue occasion… the official welcoming of a new member. I recall that day fondly and, I can now say, it is just as special when you are the one welcoming someone in to the club. With all the Rotary business taken care of for the day, we moved on to having a lively lunch before welcoming our guest speaker to the podium.

Dr. Joanna Carmichael is the Founder & CEO of the Kalyana Centre (formerly The Center for Oneness) in Narberth, Pennsylvania. Her background includes 26 years in the nursing field (including psychiatric nursing) along with over 20 years of clinical experience in the pharmaceutical research industry. During that time she committed herself to simultaneous studies in Holistic Health, Metaphysics, Divinity, Yoga, and Ayurveda resulting in two doctoral degrees which has given her a well-rounded perspective on health and healing and its intimate relationship to spirituality.

Her desire to create a place of beauty, healing and transformation where people can come to experience a variety of modalities in Alternative Medicine resulted from an intention that began when she left the pharmaceutical industry permanently in 2008 and opened the centre in September 2009. "Starting this Centre has been a dream come true," said Carmichael. "My intention to do this at a time where we need healing on all levels became manifest... I had the vision and now the vision has me." It is here where she educates people with regard to meditation, yoga, and ayurveda to help people primarily with the one thing that plagues us all... stress.

Carmichael's belief in the interconnectedness between physiology, psychology and spirituality and the need for conventional as well as complementary modalities provides a vast array of choices by which the individual can begin their journey into healing. Her background in both the hard sciences and in alternative medicine is a combination that allows for a much more holistic approach to the problems of individuals. Being able to seamlessly combine the two is something that few have been able to accomplish and understanding the limitations of both is a powerful tool to apply to the care of her clients.

Also of note is that this is not just all business and profit for Carmichael. This is a deeply held passion and something that she offers, in part, as a service to the community through a free community meditation program which she offers every Monday and Wednesday (Thursday with another practitioner) from 6:00 – 6:30 pm at the Centre. During these open sessions, attendees are invited to decompress from the day's activities and connect with like-minded people for a half hour of meditation with the overall objective being that "through meditation we are also tapping into the wisdom of our soul, where we can experience the field of infinite potential, creativity, health and wisdom."

It is because of people like Dr. Carmichael that I do my best to keep an open mind and listen to the perspectives that may be radically different from my own. Sometimes my views don't change while other times I am willing to accept the merits of some alternatives. This also demonstrates the importance of Rotary in exposing people to ideas, professions, and individuals that they wouldn't normally come across during the course of their day.

Change Is Good

———

For the second day in a row I was off to a Rotary meeting. The reason for my Rotary double down was to hear the guest speaker presenting at the Rotary Club of Philadelphia. Not only was I interested in what he had to say but I was also the one who introduced him to the opportunity earlier in the year.

In Rotary, as many of you know, we do our best to remain neutral when it comes to politics. This is a rule that I respect and abide by no matter what my views are on a particular subject. However, I fully support the discussion of ideas and the sharing of opinions as to the best solutions for problems that we face both in our club and in the community. It is for this reason that I set up the date for Terry Tracy to open up a dialogue with my fellow Rotarians over lunch at The Union League of Philadelphia.

I previously met Terry at a Commonwealth Club event in center city and was immediately impressed with his reasonable views and how his background would offer a unique perspective to the position of Controller in the City of Brotherly Love. As Rotarians we all bring different abilities and talents to the table to serve each other and the community and I believe that we should look for those same traits in those running for office. His experience running retail stores throughout North America for major multinational fashion brands grants him with exceptional ability to view the city through a lens of global appeal and appreciation for the creative management necessary to spur growth in tough times.

I can hear some of you commenting now about neutrality and party politics. Rest assured, Terry abided by the 4 Way Test throughout his discussion.

- **It is the truth?** He stuck to the facts and was completely honest in his background and opinions.
- **Is it fair to all concerned?** He did not venture into conjecture and made no mention of party politics.

- **Will it build good will and better friendship?** In a time when partisan politics is running rampant, the meeting ended with complements from Rotarians across the political spectrum.
- **Will it be beneficial to all concerned?** Regardless of location, the race for controller is often overlooked. This brought focus to a position that has a great impact on the health of the city but regularly receives little attention. All benefited from the awareness of this important position.

Just because someone is in politics and/or is a member of one party or another, it doesn't mean that neutrality can't be achieved. One's personal views will always color your perspective but it shouldn't prevent us from seeing both sides of a political race or a discussion in general. In fact, you could be surprise by what you see. Who knows, maybe your opinion will change. Maybe change is something we need.

Penny For Your Thoughts

———

It was classification talk time this week at the Rotary Club of Bala Cynwyd – Narberth as we learned a little bit more about our newest member, and our new Vice President, Penny Hughes. Penny is thriving in her second career as a banker at Bryn Mawr Trust and after opening a new branch in Bala Cynwd she made her way to our club earlier this year. Transitioning from hair stylist to banker is not a scenario that you hear often but, having known Penny for some time now, it makes perfect sense.

Bryn Mawr Trust is a bank that I know well as I grew up in Bryn Mawr just down the street from the bank's original location (still there today). My family has been at that bank for decades and I plan on transitioning my accounts over there at some point in the near future. I consider the current location of my accounts as the consequence of youthful naivety.

Penny, who serves as Branch Manager and Vice President at the Bank, is the embodiment of why I plan on moving my finances to that institution. It is the personal attention, intelligence, and a common sense approach that is unparalleled in a national institution setting. Anything and everything can be handled through the various departments at the bank in the same manner whether it is a simple banking need, loans/mortgages, investments, insurance, and various other needs.

Penny's journey at Bryn Mawr Trust is one that is fueled by her intelligence, people person personality, hard work, and inspired by her philosophy on life passed down from her Grandmother. Working her way up from a part time teller to a VP and Branch Manager, Penny is the embodiment of the American Dream and she is proof that even if you do something for 20+ years doesn't mean you can't change and be successful in a completely different line of work. And now, of course, that transition has brought her to Rotary.

Penny's exemplary attributes are why we have decided to appoint her as our club's Vice President. I look forward to working with her in the years ahead as I know she will bring the same fervor and love of people and service to Rotary as she does to her job. As a small club we have to watch every penny and now we can watch what great things can be accomplished by one Penny in particular.

A Lion In The Classroom

———

Experience is one of the most powerful teaching tools that we have to offer to others and we all learned many lessons at one of our weekly Rotary meetings in particular. There are people that you meet during your life that you will always remember the stories they told about the life they have lived. Jack Binstead is someone whose life has impacted countless people and continues to influence more and more people every day.

Jack spent 27 years as an English teacher at Overbrook High School trying to bridge the educational gap that still exists in many of our urban schools today. In his decades in the classroom he experienced the highs and lows few experience in their chosen profession. He recalled the countless students who have gone on to become authors, artists, singers, professional athletes, politicians, CEOs, and even a movie star which was tempered by the fact that, during his career, he experienced the loss of 45 students who didn't live to see graduation.

Unfortunately, all too often the tragedy of 45 commonly outweighs the success of hundreds and is used to generalize the students that attend this and similar schools. It is important to remember that greatness is not limited by race or the economy; it is determined by desire, passion, and education. What we need are teachers that can kindle desire, inspire passion, and motivate students to value education. Jack was one of those teachers in the classroom and is still one of those teachers outside of the confines of academia.

Jack's passion for education is evident when he talks about the many students and experiences he had at Overbrook and his passion for service shines through when he speaks of his long tenure with the Bala Cynwyd – Narberth Lions. Whereas his served a community of students for many years, his focus on service now extends to the entire community. Similar to Rotary in many ways Lions are a service centric organization that follows a simple principle, "Whenever a Lions club gets together, problems get smaller. And communities get better."

Locally and internationally there have been many instances where both organizations have worked together to improve communities and help solve common problems. Just as when you enter many towns throughout this country with a Rotary and a Lions sign along the road, we work together in each community. Sometimes it takes a Lion. Sometimes it takes a Rotarian. Sometimes it takes a Kiwanis. Sometimes it takes a Mason. The most important thing is that we get people involved, we work together, and we all do what we can to solve some of the problems facing our local communities and the international community.

In this drive to do good we have to be open and we must communicate. This is not a matter of "I'm better than you" or "this is better than that". We are all different organizations but we can still have a common voice and in order to accomplish this we have to remember that communication is key, the effectiveness of which all comes down to what you say and how you say it. This is one of the tenants that Jack taught to his students and it is something that we should all keep in mind as it is something that can easily be forgotten.

Simply put, don't use your words to segregate service, use them to unite a community. Rotarians, invite a Lion to speak at your club. Lions, invite a Rotarian to speak at your club. Learn from all your experiences and find ways to help each other as well as the community and objectives you have in common. Remember, it's all about "service above self"!

Brace Yourself To Be Kicked In The Fannie

Interesting discussions abound every week during our regular Rotary meeting. The diversity both in our members and our guests makes for a wide variety of views and varying levels of passion about any given topic. With so much going on in the country and world today there is an endless stream of talking points to spur impassioned dialogues.

Our guest this week, Matthew D. Weglarz, brought to the forefront one such topic when he discussed the ever changing lending market and the possible implications if Fannie Mae and Freddie Mac are allowed to fold. Most notable of the probable outcomes would be the privatization of the mortgage industry and the subsequent elimination of terms extending beyond 15 years. This would be in addition to the increased interest rates that would reflect levels that haven't been seen in over 30 years. Of course, these are suppositions at this point and like many events in the past we won't know the true outcome until it happens as there are too many variables to fully comprehend.

Matt, who works for Merrill Lynch Wealth Management and serves as Vice President and Resident Manager for the Philadelphia and South Jersey Regions, was very concise in his outlining the current situation that exists in the lending industry but also touched upon his own journey that shapes the way he conducts himself and treats others. The journey that lead him to his current position was not one that is commonly heard of in the executive ranks of his industry.

It is the understanding on a personal and professional level of the highs and lows that exist in life and the extremes in means that exist in society that makes Matt particularly effective in not just helping people make the right decisions but also to give perspective to the raw numbers. Many people are great with numbers but it takes a certain kind of person to see the humanity in the arithmetic. It is something that we each have inside of us, something that Matt has obviously tapped into, and something that we should all keep in mind when we go about our work.

Look for the humanity in what may seem emotionless; find the flex in the immutable; challenge what is accepted as the norm; strive to achieve greater and greater things in life. Don't just see these as ideas, see them for what they are... actions. We can see these actions in the lives of others, in people like Matt, and know that it can be done because it has been done. If you want to serve others know how to serve yourself as well.

One If By Hand, Two If By PC

Most people don't give much thought to the legibility of their own handwriting. Poor penmanship is something that we tend to only notice when we have to read a note, a form, or, all too often for some, a prescription. But on a day to day basis we really don't think about this.

As I have said before, one of the wonderful aspects of Rotary is meeting people and hearing speakers who introduce concepts and ideas that we wouldn't normally give significant consideration in our everyday lives. The importance of handwriting and the legibility thereof is something that Dr. Beverly Moskowitz has dedicated her life to for the majority of her 37 years of experience as a pediatric Occupational Therapist. In 2011, she authored the largest research study ever conducted with the primary focus placed on handwriting with her program proven to be 99.9% effective in the classroom.

During our meeting she shared with us the evidence generated from that study of why handwriting instruction still matters and how learning institutions can embed effective, efficient, measurable and fun manuscript instruction into the school day. The results, to say the least, are staggering and the need for further instruction in this simple fine motor skill is one that not only provides the basic benefit of clear written communication but it has a much longer lasting impact on the functionality and effectiveness of the written word which students carry with them throughout their lives. The ability to formulate concise thoughts and articulate them efficiently and effectively is rooted in the fundamentals of putting the tip of the pen or pencil on the paper.

This breakthrough is a result of Dr. Moskowitz's extensive real world experience as a school therapist where she has serviced more than fifteen school districts and over 60 different schools. Her broad exposure to a variety of teaching methods, administrative styles, and treatment interventions has confirmed her resolve to insure function, participation and inclusion for all students without wasting time. The result of this lifetime of experience in conjunction with her creative background has been a body of intellectual property and products that reflect current educational policy, practices and problems alongside the latest evidence and curricular demands.

In 2010, after spending years in the field as well as authoring numerous publications (including Practical Strategies for Increasing the Effectiveness, Efficiency, and Impact of your School-Based Occupational Therapy Practice) and lecturing across the country through the Bureau of Education and Research, Dr. Moskowitz launched Real OT Solutions, Inc. The company's mission, as both a service and product-oriented business is to provide consumers (therapists, teachers, parents and kids) with Effective, Efficient, Affordable and Fun solutions. Guided by evidence and literature on best practices regarding optimum function, independence and accessibility, they create tools to make kids successful, documentation fast, teachers cooperative, and parents satisfied.

I personally have little background in the field of education beyond my participation as a student and a few stints as a teaching assistant. However, I have spent the majority of my life putting pen to page which has made me who I am today. I know for a fact that the inability to accomplish this simple task is something that has a detrimental effect on the creative, processing, and overall mental abilities of an individual.

This is, in large part, why the annual survey results of incoming college freshmen outlined in the Beloit College Mindset List is so important because in 2010 it was revealed that the majority, and a large one at that, of incoming students didn't know how to write in cursive. My immediate thought is that if you can't write cursive how do you expect to read, or more accurately put decipher, something written in the hand of someone else? It just goes to show that history is not the only thing that is lost on much of the younger generations. How long before they forget the name Paul Revere (we have already forgotten Israel Bissell)? After all, kids can't even read anything written in his hand anyway.

In the end this is not just a generational disconnect but also a modern social division as well. On a screen everyone seems equal but when you put pens in people's hands there is an erosion of both confidence and the ability to communicate as well as clear evidence of the degradation that exists in the school systems. Confidence in writing breeds confidence in thought and communication. Effective communication is the great equalizer so if you want to achieve true equality in the schools you much make sure that all students can communicate.

Can A Hedge Fund Have A Heart?

―――――

Anyone who has ever watched Shark Tank can recognize when someone has it and when someone doesn't. Even with a great idea the entrepreneurial spirit is not always present. As soon as Deepta Hiremath began presenting yesterday at our Rotary meeting I could tell she had it.

Our guest speaker two weeks ago spoke about the mortgage market and the potentially drastic changes on the horizon and how the process for people to get mortgages in the future will differ from today's market. However, that doesn't address the distressed mortgages and struggling families that are already in the marketplace and are trying to find a way to get their heads above water. This is where the focus of our discussion was yesterday.

Deepta owns and operates a real estate hedge fund by the name of King Peak LLC. While that term has fallen from favor in recent years there are still people out there running hedge funds that exemplify the four way test. Those people are not focused solely on the bottom dollar but are also looking for a mutually beneficial arrangement that is fair for all parties concerned. While the objective of any business is to be profitable it doesn't mean you can't help people along the way.

It is no secret that as a result of the crash in 2008, over-leveraged banks have been selling off second mortgages at drastic discounts in order to recoup guaranteed money which can be funneled back into the capital reserve. Who buys these mortgages? Debt collectors and entrepreneurs like Deepta.

While credit collectors will commonly flip the paper using high volume deals without any thought given to the lives and livelihoods that those mortgages represent, Deepta invests more than her money into these transactions. She invests her time, her energy, and her heart. Deepta focuses on the mortgages that commonly have the most devastating impact… second mortgages.

Due to the steep discount at which she purchased the paper, it opens up the opportunity to help and try to work with homeowners so that they can remain homeowners. She evaluates many of these mortgages on an individual and very personal basis and tries to find the best solution for everyone. Given the margins and the huge number of buyers, Deepta is almost guaranteed a profit. She doesn't need to take the extra step but she does because she knows that what she holds in her hand is more than just paper.

It is part of the American dream to have the spouse, the house, and two and a half kids but sometimes we all need a little help to maintain that reality especially in these still trying times. As Rotarians we try to do right by others and ourselves every second of every day and while sometimes we may falter and show our human shortcomings it helps to have a business plan which helps us to live those principals. We can learn a lot from Deepta as well as other intelligent and driven entrepreneurs like her which will not just help to reinforce the Rotary principals but also as a reminder to ourselves of what can be done when we embody those principals.

Teaching Zen On The Tennis Court

For most of us, no matter how much we enjoy our job we look forward to leaving our work at the office and forgetting about all the ins and outs of our weekly tasks as soon as we get home (or as soon as you walk into the next room for those of you who work at home). Of course, there are some people who are lucky enough to have found a job that really isn't work. They are driven people who enjoy every day and live their passion.

This is the life of Carlos Girola who developed his passion growing up in Argentina and now serves as the Tennis Director at the Llanerch Country Club in Havertown, Pennsylvania. Carlos doesn't work; he lives his passion and gets paid for it. At yesterday's Rotary meeting we had the pleasure of hearing him speak with such admiration, respect, and passion for how he makes a living that I couldn't help but be impressed with his lifelong pursuit of the sport and desire to impart the love of the game in others.

According to Carlos, some of his greatest and most satisfying professional accomplishments include earning his USPTA Pro 1 certification, teaching wheelchair tennis for three years, building a tennis center in South Africa in 1991, and introducing tennis as recreational therapy for mentally ill patients. He started teaching tennis in 1981 at age 17 when his coach offered him a position at a club in Argentina. "I became a teaching pro because I love tennis and I make people of all ages happy by teaching and promoting the game," he says.

Carlos enjoys every day on the court with his students. No matter what the age, ability, background, or build he believes that everyone can experience the almost transcendental state that all tennis players experience whether they are professionals, amateurs, or novices. All it takes is some basic abilities and techniques, all of which can be taught, in order for someone to experience the Zen of a long rally.

It is this perspective and appreciation of the sport and how it applies to everyone, not just the enthusiasts, which differentiates Carlos from many other teachers that I have come across in various sports. Not everyone has the talent, drive, and unwillingness to lose that the greats of the game have (he mentioned Bjorn Borg, Roger Federer, and Pete Sampras as prime examples of this) and you don't need them. All it takes is an interest and a basic understanding of the game in order to develop a lifelong enthusiasm for the court.

Unlike many athletic endeavors, tennis is one that is adaptable to the time in someone's life. Whether age, injury, or simply a lack of time, these can all be taken into account so that the sport remains ever present in life. Carlos is able to break down the basics of the game and the needs of the player (contrary to the wants that we all have) in order to maintain a level that will satisfy the need to play and keep the enthusiasm for the sport in their heart.

Professionals like Carlos are the reason why the US Open is the highest drawing annual sporting event in the country. As is the case with many sports there are many knowledgeable professional with which you can speak and learn about the game. However, there aren't nearly as many great teachers who can impart that knowledge and enthusiasm in others in a way that can be applied to the court. It is teachers like Carlos Girola who are truly advancing the sport and serving as the catalyst for the passion that tennis needs to thrive in this county.

Fiction Takes A Back Seat To Reality

———

Every once in a while in your life you meet someone who is truly an astounding individual who has lived a life that you only read about in books or see in the movies (or in a beer commercial). And sometimes it takes a second meeting to realize how remarkable someone is. This was the case when Dr. Liann Francisco was invited back to our Rotary club as a presenter.

Liann is a woman who has lived two lives. After a successful career working with the government, primarily with the military but also included assignments with the Pentagon and US Marshall Service, she is now dedicating herself to electronic security and surveillance in the private sector. However, this was only the beginning of her entrepreneurial efforts as she has recently ventured into the field of aviation. I guess you could say she is revisiting the aviation industry but no one, at least anyone I know of, would pay to take a ride on Con Air (Liann was the engineer behind the design of the US Marshall's primary method of air transportation… not the Nicholas Cage version).

Of course, you can't accomplish as much as she has done and flipped her life upside down and inside out as many times as she has without being a highly motivated and intellectually curious individual. Even in her spare time, Liann has pursued her pilot's license, dive master certification, EMT certification, and is an USCG Boat Captain as well as a Black Belt in Tie Kwon Do. If that weren't enough she is also an avid drummer and ham radio operator (if you don't know what that is ask your parents or look it up).

I never knew all this when I first met Liann a few weeks ago when she came as a guest of our club's president, Dr. Sherman Leis. We spoke a little about her former life working with the government and a little about her recent venture into aviation but nothing really beyond the type of conversation that one would have when first meeting another professional at a Rotary meeting for the first time. This is a perfect example of the fact that truly amazing people won't say they are amazing… their brilliance only comes out when you take the time to get to know them.

This is also a prime reason why all clubs should welcome the people who accompany members to a meeting. Don't let any preconceptions dictate reality. Great men and women are around us every day; it is up to us to discover their brilliance.

The same can be said for your fellow Rotarians any why it is so important for us all to give presentations not only about our professions but also about our passions and interests. We are quite the diverse group when you sit down and think about it and I have known many successful businesspeople in my life whose talents shown through in their other endeavors more so than their day to day jobs. Few people are able to combine the two, whether due to lack of courage, opportunity, or means, but sometimes you come across someone who has been able to do just that, someone like Liann.

It's safe to say that she definitely gives the guy in the Dos Equis beer commercial a run for his money. Oh wait, that's right, he isn't real. It just goes to show that if you pay attention, get out there and meet people, you will find individuals that put fiction to shame.

What Impact Do You Have In This World?

Sometimes we all need a reminder. We go to our Rotary meeting every week, we discuss different projects and listen to speakers, but we need to be reminded every now and then about the real power that can be found in Rotary. All too often we get caught up in the minutia and forget about the way that Rotary has changed and continues to impact lives around the world.

This is why I always enjoy the meetings that bring our District Governor to our club. Our current Governor, Charles E. Streitwieser, brought his years of experience and his dedication to our meeting yesterday and we are all better for it. Since joining Rotary in 1996 he has been a driving force in our district and a tremendous influence both within Rotary and in the community. As a member of the Rotary Club of West Chester, his most gratifying assignments have been to serve on his club's Task Force for Community Needs Assessment and its New Member Mentors Committee. These efforts helped the club to grow to become the largest club in our District.

Charles is not only cognizant of the local impact that Rotary has on changing lives but he is acutely aware of the global importance of Rotary. Most notably, he pointed out, is the role that Rotary plays in transcending religion, politics, and geographic barriers. Whether it is mediating conflicts along the Israel-Palestine boarder, unifying humanitarian efforts between India and Pakistan, or taking part in global initiatives through the United Nations, Rotary has stood the test of time and continues to elevate its reputation as an organization that promotes peace, cooperation, and unity among all the citizens of this world.

These are the things that we commonly lose sight of in our daily lives and our weekly meetings. Our international and district officers are the people that keep our eyes open to the world around us in a way that is unbiased and altruistic in nature. The immediate impact of our work is not just felt within our own community. It takes action to create action and Rotary serves as the catalyst in making waves in this world.

However, the impact of our work is not just felt by others. Our work and the work of our fellow Rotarians, impacts our own lives in a way that is difficult to measure. All of us who feel this passion and see the good that is being done through this organization that we all care so deeply about are bound together. We are individuals but we are also one, we are Rotary.

It is this community that we constantly nurture and the work that springs forth from this connectivity that can serve and should serve as the driving force behind attracting new members. We all have something valuable to contribute regardless of age or profession. Just like any other family, Rotary must grow and in doing so nurture and guide the lives and actions of younger Rotarians. Despite the ever increasing connectivity, the world is still a vast place and Rotary extends a helping hand into every corner of this planet. This is an experience that cannot be kept to ourselves and we look forward to giving everyone the opportunity of being that hand of help.

This is the impact that Rotary has on the world. We can change lives and, by doing so change, the world. And we can share this opportunity with others. We all exist in this world but how many of us take action and decide to live? This is what we can achieve through Rotary.

One Man Can Change The World

Since our club's founding in 1926 we had never had such a distinguished guest speaker as we had yesterday when Rotary International Past President Wilfred Wilkinson honored us with his presence. In attendance were fellow Rotarians from throughout the region comprising of hundreds, if not over a thousand years of service. It was not only an inspiring but a humbling experience. Seeing so many great men and women united in Rotary is an amazing experience to be a part of.

The afternoon flew by so quickly that it is hard to recall all of the details but there are a few clear moments and emotions that will forever resonate in my own life. Past President Wilkinson's remarks were full of not only a passion for Rotary and service but a love for people and the impact that our work has had on this world. Having traveled around the world, he has seen the many faces that have benefited from the efforts of Rotarians and he has seen the diversity that is represented in Rotary clubs around the globe. No matter how different we all may seem, we are all connected to one another through Rotary and through a desire for peace.

In reading about Past President Wilkinson's achievements and his tenure at the helm of Rotary International there was one quote that I came across that summed up my impression of this great man as the embodiment of the Rotary motto "service above self". During his address at the Rotary Convention in Los Angeles, California on June 15th, 2008 he said the following:

> "One of the first questions I had from the staff when I was nominated was what I wanted as my RI theme. I was all ready with my answer. I said my theme would be *Rotary Shares*. Because to me, these words captured all that was good about Rotary and Rotarians. Because to me, Rotary is about sharing. It's about sharing our time, every week in our meetings with our fellow members and with our communities and with people throughout the world. It's about sharing our expertise, our talents, and our resources in countless ways. It's about sharing what we have, with our fellow Rotarians and with those in need. That's what I told my district governors, when we began this Rotary year. But now I know better. Yes, *Rotary Shares* means all that, but it means so much more. It means every one of you and every single Rotarian in every Rotary country working together. Working with dedication and working with love, working for a better, safer, healthier, and more peaceful world."

This is what it means to be a Rotarian. This is what we all strive to do each and every day of our lives. This is how we continue to improve our communities, this is how we touch the lives of people we have never met in places we have never been, this is how we change the world. One person, one club, one community, one seemingly insignificant action, one small project, one life impacted can make all the difference in this world.

Let our work be enhanced through Rotary. Let us work together to serve our communities. Let our actions, through Rotary, be magnified 100 fold. It is in this spirit, with all of us together as one community, that we launched our raffle to benefit The Rotary Club of Bala Cynwyd – Narberth's

Community Educational Initiative which supports children from West Philadelphia schools through various programs and projects.

The Paul Harris Fellow Award Raffle is an idea that, to the knowledge of everyone I have spoken with, has never been done in the history of our great organization. By selling tickets for a prize that is unique to Rotary, every Rotarian and every club is sharing in the support of those school children in need in our community. Each ten dollars collected has a Rotarian's name and carries with it their passion for service and their desire to improve the community. The success of this program will be shared with the holders of the two hundred tickets while the credit goes to every Rotarian for supporting us in this endeavor and making it possible to accomplish such great work.

It all starts with an idea just like Rotary started as an idea by one man, Paul Harris. Ideas come and go but those which are met with passion and supported by the community quickly take hold and begin to bring about change. One idea can certainly impact a community while some ideas can change the world. This world needs great ideas and this world needs great men. We need, especially during this time in history, passionate people dedicated to making this world a better, more peaceful place. We need people like Past President Wilfred Wilkinson.

Does it promote GOOD WILL and BETTER FRIENDSHIP?

Offering Guidance And Assistance To ALL Rotarians

Either Get On The Cart Or Go To The Mattresses!

Membership is a major concern for most, if not all, Rotary clubs and new ideas seem to be presented on a regular basis on how to attract new members (especially young professionals in their 20's and 30's). Unfortunately, many clubs can hear Eric Idle's chanting from "Monty Python and the Holy Grail" ringing in their ears. What we must do in response is to persevere and let people know "I'm getting better… I feel happy."

I am not going to waste your time saying I have the answer and I am not going to tell you what is the right way or wrong way to attract members. The purpose of this article is to help you organize and set the ground work for an effective membership drive during next Rotary year which is approaching fast.

Many of the building blocks outlined below mirror the fundamentals reviewed previously because that is exactly what they are… fundamentals. The following seven steps have been specifically selected as they can be applied to all clubs regardless of geography, size, and financial health.

- **Know Your Club** – By knowing the members of your club, their professions, their capabilities, and their interests you can better focus the direction of the club not only with regard to service projects but also in how to proceed in pursuing members and how the responsibilities for that task would be best divided.
- **Review Demographics** – This is not only the other half of the equation in finding the most appropriate service projects but it is also essential in properly pursuing members. Determine the average age and income of the community. Understand what kind of businesses are the most prevalent. Find out what kind of events and speakers garner the greatest attendance in the area. Basically, know the people around you and coordinate your membership initiatives accordingly.

- **Be Ready To Sell** – Just like any sales force, make sure your members are informed. Make sure there is a working knowledge in place regarding all aspects of Rotary and specifically what the club does for the community. Don't be timid about letting people know you are a Rotarian… this can be achieved simply by making sure your members wear their Rotary pin every day and encouraging members to be open and ready to talk about Rotary when someone asks.

- **Focus On Service, Not Food** – Now that your clubs service efforts are in sync with both the abilities of the membership and the needs of the community, invite perspective members to participate. We can't lose track of why we are Rotarians. We are not a club for foodies. We are a service organization. After all, it's not about the dealership, it's about the car.

- **Be Honest and Be Flexible** – When a prospect asks you a question be up front with them… we each need to be the embodiment of the four way test. At the same time, speak up and encourage new and perspective members to do the same. If something isn't working for you discuss it with your fellow Rotarians because, in this instance, silence is the absence of truth. This facilitates an ongoing evaluation of the club… do you still meet at the best time, place, day? Are their new skills available to the club or any other service projects that a new person is particularly passionate about? Make sure everyone is part of the process.

- **Communication and Networking** – How does your club best communicate with one another? How do you communicate with other clubs? You have to know the basics of communications. If no one in your club uses social media then it is useless to post information only pertinent to members on Facebook. With that said, every club should have all lines of communication available to members and prospects ranging from a mailing address to a twitter account. Communication is essential to the networking capabilities of the club and is the key to the overall structure of the community and media relations efforts. The club needs to be open to the public because where else do your members come from?

- **Make Your Presence Known** – Rotary has proven that good PR leads to an increase in membership. Just as each member's voice should be heard within the club so too should the club's voice be heard in the community. In order to magnify the club's efforts a single point of contact, a public relations chair (if you have not done so thus far) should be appointed and all members (officers in particular) should support their efforts by continuously communicating with the chair. A record of your club's service, achievements, and guest speakers (past, present, and future of each) should be readily available to everyone, Rotarians and non Rotarians (or as I like to say Rotarians and future Rotarians) by way of your club's social media accounts and, when possible, through traditional media placements. And remember, when it comes to events and announcements, don't underestimate the power of a press release.

Is this list perfect? No. There is always something that can be added and there are always essential details that need to be tailored to your club. Are these steps guaranteed to work? No. But they will provide you with the basics. This is not a how to article; this is a way to formulate your own plan. What if it doesn't work? Try something else. Are we going to give up and let the pessimistic voices win? Heck NO!

We represent the community, we represent Rotary International, and we represent our fellow Rotarians. We are not a group that simply gives up because we can see what happens when we persevere… ask yourself the following questions, how many cases of Polio have been reported this year? How many cases were there before 1985?

The work speaks for itself. We must rise and continue to fight. And if all else fails, go to the mattresses!

Don't Forget The Mint On The Pillow!

———

Taking time to step back, breathe, and evaluate is sometimes the hardest thing for each of us to do. To a certain extent, this is something that we strive to do every week at Rotary by discussing many of the larger campaigns that continue to impact the world. We are constantly exploring the ways that we can contribute to those endeavors as well as local projects that have an immediate effect on our own community. When we find an idea in sync with our objectives and our vocational abilities we work on the details of implementation and construct a broad stroke plan to get things moving. Essentially, by stepping back and looking at the big picture we are able to delve into the details and find our way to best serve the community and contribute to Rotary in general.

Where many of us get tripped up is in the effectiveness of our club and the frequently overlooked foundational aspects of our club as well as its attributes, objectives, and goals. The reason this is commonly overlooked is simple… with so many worthwhile campaigns we don't want to stop and take care of the basic housekeeping.

This doesn't mean that anything has been neglected or needs to be discontinued. It is simply a status update, an evaluation of where we stand, and a means of cleaning out inefficiency and ensuring that the clubs activities are in harmony with members and best serve Rotary and the community. Once the existing structure of the club has been surveyed, deficiencies can be addressed and new goals can be established.

When was the last time you asked members to complete a club assessment survey or evaluated the needs of your own community (you would be surprised at how quickly this can change)?

These are the first tasks that need to be completed and this should be done on a regular basis. By taking the time to cover these basics, you can properly guide your club in a direction that not only increases the potential success of you club but also of the community. It also brings to light that some of the things your club may be good at are covering up many shortcomings… you may be able to raise a lot of money but membership is down, you may have a great reputation but your communications and public relations are almost nonexistent, you may have a wide range of speakers but lack vocational diversity.

What are the demographics of you community (economy, education, age, etc.)?When was the last time you did a membership survey? Are you actively inviting local business owners to attend a meeting? Do you invite all of your guest speakers to become members? How frequently do your members attend meetings at other clubs?

It is time to delve into the details… simple surveys based on these questions are what help to truly refocus the membership. Having a greater understanding of community demographics and, therefore, the needs of the community in conjunction with the club's membership demographics can, many times, be quite eye opening. These two surveys alone can be great tools in assisting the club in filling gaps in vocation, age, education, etc. In the end, we want our club to represent the community and in order to do that we need to have a membership that reflects the neighborhood(s), has speakers that are appealing to the community, make sure that people feel welcomed and comfortable, and have projects and goals that the community can not only appreciate but want to contribute. Understanding demographics can go a long way in achieving these goals and ensuring the ongoing success of both campaign and membership objectives.

The last bit of strategy that needs to be in place is an effective public relations and communication plan. Changes to you club mean nothing if no one knows about it. Make sure your club has a presence on social media, make sure you notify the community about speakers, make sure other clubs within your Rotary district and the officers know of your club (this is especially important for small clubs), and don't be afraid to send press releases to the media about both upcoming events and write ups of past events (including your weekly speakers).

Don't underestimate the importance of making your presence known to the community. Remember, people tend not to notice that a hotel room has been cleaned and the bed turned down until they see the mint on the pillow.

Don't Be Intimidated By A Perfect 10

As Rotarians, like Dudley Moore, we all strive for that perfect 10. Sometimes the results can be as beautiful as Bo Derek. However, they can sometimes more closely resemble something that Dave Letterman recites around midnight.

What we need to keep in mind is that the perfect 10 is a purely subjective number. What may be a perfect list of goals for one club may be disastrous for another. The following list contains what I see as catalysts to further the impact and ignite the passion within my own club:

- 50% Increase in Membership: As a smaller club this is a goal that does not require a huge number of new members. It is generally anticipated that Rotary clubs will lose 10% of their membership every year. As a general rule of thumb, clubs should set the goal to compensate for that loss and add an additional 5 members. Our goal this year will be to add 9 members.

- 150 Hours of Community Service: This figure should be derived from the current membership total. 10 hours of service per member per year is a very low number and should be easily achievable. Of course, this excludes the work that officers put in and organizational hours. This should only include hours at events, hours serving the community.

- 12 New Club Banners: Exchanging banners with other clubs is frequently overlooked by Rotarians however it is essential in strengthening the connections within the Rotary community. We are all working toward the same goals and we can all offer help to other clubs and work with other clubs on projects. This is particularly important for smaller clubs as we can frequently be overlooked. Get out there and visit other clubs… 1 per month should be the absolute minimum and remember not to duplicate existing banners.

- Networking Events and Local Business Outreach: You have to give something to get something and by providing the community with a networking event and a place to promote their business you can, generally speaking, gain new members. That is reality; you must demonstrate the value that Rotary brings to their business and, by actively involving them, allow the value of service to develop within the new Rotarian. We must promote growth within the individual if we are going to actualize the growth of our club and Rotary as a whole.

- New Member 1st Year Program: Give your new members some guidance by outlining some basic goals for them to reach during their first year. Encourage them to visit other clubs and collecting banners, give them the opportunity to exceed 10 hours of community service, have them bring 10 guests during the course of the year, make sure they give a presentation to the club, send them to RLI to complete Level I. These are some of the basics that will certainly set them up for success. Also recommended is to ensure that their mentors accompany them along the way. Don't forget to acknowledge those who have met or exceeded the goals.

- Establishing a Rotaract Club: This has been an ongoing project. This is the year that we are going to get it done. Our focus has been a little off in the past but now we know the right department and the right approach to take. This is a case where we need to make our presence known not only to potentially new Rotarians but also future Rotarians because our present has little value if we don't have a future.

- Connecting with After School Programs: How can your club enhance the current after school programs in your area? What better way to impact the next generation in your community than to instill the values of Rotary in each of them and reinforce the fact that they are a valuable part of our community. By being of service to them they will, in turn, be of service to others but setting the example for their community and their contemporaries.

- Expanding the Literacy Program: Our current program consists of handing out dictionaries to third graders in the local area with recent expansion of the program to consist of an essay contest in those same classrooms. Don't get me wrong, this is a great program but we can do more and we need to do more to remain in their minds. Start off early by reading to second grade classrooms ("Rotary Clubs Help People" is the perfect book for this project) and expand the essay contest by implementing it as a multi-year endeavor that follows the children as they grow. This can easily be spread across four years by having the children write about the four way test one item at a time. So, instead of one year when they are in third grade you can have an annual presence in their lives for six consecutive years (with the possibility of longer continuous involvement if the aforementioned goals are achieved).

- Honoring Veterans and Service Members: Simply put, pay respect to the heroes in your community. Twice a year, the weeks of Veteran's Day and Memorial Day, invite a veteran or active service member to speak to your club. Let them choose the topic but make sure to honor them for their service as well. Make sure you let them know that they are always welcome at Rotary and their fellow veterans and service members are welcome as well. Rotary is a safe place, a place of peace, a place of service to others. They have already served us so let us return that service to them.

- Website and PR Overhaul: This is where I am personally going to focus my efforts this year. I am not going to speak much on the PR side as it has already been discussed previously at length. However, what was not really discussed was the importance of having your own functional website. It doesn't have to be pretty (or a perfect 10) but it has to be functional, informative, and look good. Make sure the content is up to date, a schedule is available, list where and when you meet, and have a way for prospects and fellow Rotarians to connect with officers of the club.

Lists are nothing but a sequence of numbers if no action is taken. Careful thought and consideration must be taken to ensure that the members of your club and the officers are on the same page. Whether by vocation, connections they may have, personal motivation, or simply enough time to see it through, match the initiatives that your club has with the member that is most likely to succeed at achieving that goal. And if someone runs out of gas be there to help them push the project forward.

Who Helps You Focus Your Efforts?

Every week, or nearly every week for some, Rotarians gather for their weekly Rotary meeting. Every day there is something that needs to be taken care of or addressed to keep the club running as smoothly as possible. Emails, phone calls, meetings, mailings, filings, promotions, etc. are all part of what keeps things going behind the scenes.

It is a constantly regenerating list that is without end and it is the officers that take charge of these tasks. It is a full time job that these people do without pay and they are duties that are, generally speaking, ones that no one enjoys doing. When was the last time you looked forward to stuffing envelopes? How many of you eagerly await emails that ask for everything under the sun and you have to be the one to consolidate the fundraising efforts into a concise message/focus?

Admittedly, I enjoy both to varying degrees, but I am also incredibly odd. Most of the people I talk to basically run in the opposite direction when they are asked to assist in one or both of these matters while the ones that agree to help do so begrudgingly. And of course there are the ones that ignore the request and, instead, add another item to the to do list (these are the people that insist that whatever it is needs to be taken care of as soon as possible).

Since when did volunteering with a community centric organization require a political background? Pork belly charity seems to be the name of the game and implementation without financial forethought can run rampant if left unchecked. With the demands placed on the clubs and on the people behind them, it is astounding that anything gets done. Don't get me wrong, this is by no means a blanket statement and should not be taken as a deterrent to either those thinking about joining or those considering taking a leadership role as there are many clubs that run very smoothly and the members understand both the limitations and opportunities within which they must operate.

The purpose of this article is for those who are members and are proud of their affiliation to consider the bigger picture and not to just think about what you want to see your club accomplish but to consider the other factors at play. First and foremost, does the project address a need that exists in the community or is it simply something that you want to do? If a need can be established, address the following questions and dig a little deeper. Does your club have the means to see the project through to the end both financially and with regard to the time commitment? Is the project the best use of the club's time and finances?

Everyone has good ideas and the occasional great one but we can't be everything to everyone. While it is hard to sometimes have to let go of an idea or project, it is something that needs to be done every once in a while in order to ensure that the greatest possible impact can be made with the resources at hand. This is not a foreign concept and I'm sure that this is not the first time that you have heard those questions but they are definitely worth repeating as they are frequently forgotten.

I have experienced the wide spectrum of how operations are handled as well as the expectations that members have of their club and the officers. While one is easier to deal with than the other, the motivation to contribute is not dependent on ease of operation. It all comes down to passion. If you maintain your passion to give back to the community, help others, and be a part of something greater than yourself you will put up with almost anything in order to see the impact that your club can have on those around you.

Remember that those who take on a larger role are people who want to see things get done. They are not there as a barrier, all they are trying to do is to make sure the proposals made are in the best interests of the membership, the club, and the community. If you can assist them in any small way I encourage you to do so. Whether it is by assisting with some of the aforementioned tasks, helping streamline a process or system, or general things here and there any and all support is appreciated. Or, if you are unable to do any of the above, take the time to thank them for their service.

This is why we put service above self. This is how we improve ourselves while we improve our community and why we take the good along with the not so good. It is just that simple.

PR CPR

Just a few thoughts stemming from a district meeting I had last night in King of Prussia....

Public relations and communications are an important part of any successful company or organization and Rotary is no different. Too often, this is something that is overlooked both at the club and on the district level but that perspective is slowly changing and those of us in District 7450 are doing our part by encouraging our fellow Rotarians to make that mental transition. However, this is a transition that is going to take a lot of time and a lot of energy.

The mentality that exists within most clubs, particularly smaller ones, is that the focus needs to be entirely on the service side of things. Those items or tasks that are necessary to promote the club itself are secondary. This is why many of us struggle with both membership and fundraising.

Unfortunately, there is also the generational and technological disconnect that exists in the membership which hinders the adoption both of methods and strategies essential for growth. Obviously, things need to change and they need to do so in a big way. The question is how do we implement such change into a system and a population that is hesitant to embrace a new way of holistic service to the community, club, district, and one another?

Change needs to be a step by step process not a mandate. A perfect example is social media. Many members are uninterested in having a Facebook profile and don't see the need for one. The task then becomes to create the need. Show them why it would be a good thing to have in their lives both personally and regarding their Rotary involvement.

Maybe they want to see all the pictures of their grandkids, maybe they want to meet new people, maybe they want to get more involved in their service but are unable to make a regular time commitment. Demonstrate the value it can have in their own lives and they will better understand the need for the club to have a presence as well. It is not a guarantee but you will, most likely, reach at least a few members with this approach.

Traditional media is also something that needs to be high on the priority list and while it may take greater effort it can also carry with it a greater impact on your club's exposure. Most clubs, large and small, promote large events and service projects to the local main stream media but that is only part of the story. Clubs need to write about and disseminate information regarding the weekly guest speakers as well as the induction of new members at the very least. Remember, if your club's name is seen one time it's a good thing but when people see your club regularly then you are entering into the realm of PR. This is when you are seen as an integral part of the community.

There are numerous other topics and details that can be discussed around the subject of PR and communications and many of which have already been addressed. But, for now, I will leave you with the above topics for consideration and I encourage you to get involved by finding new ways to promote your club and to promote Rotary. There is no question that we do great work as Rotarians but sometimes they can go by the wayside if no one knows about them so let your voice and your club's voice be heard.

Rotarians of the Round Table

This essay stems from an interesting post by J Armando Jeronymo, a Rotarian in Brazil. He posed the following question and details on the discussion board in the Official Rotary International Group on LinkedIn:

> "What historical or fictional characters would you invite to join your club? I had this funny thought a few days ago and decided to share it. Which real character from local or universal history or fictional from books, movies, TV sitcoms or even from your folklore would you like to see in your club? Please let us have the character, the source and your reason for inviting."

This is a fascinating question to consider and the responses from around the world have contained many powerful and influential names in world history. Of course, this got me thinking as well and after about a week of mulling over the countless possibilities I pulled together a list containing mostly overlooked people that would bring an interesting dynamic to Rotary. As you will see, the twenty names below are eclectic to say the least but all offer an interesting perspective.

To begin the list we will look at one of the basic needs that many clubs struggle with… funding. Since any substantial amount of funds is nothing more than a fantasy for most clubs, I have selected two fictional Rotarians to fill this need. While his actions are not "beneficial to all concerned" I think we could guide Robin Hood in the right direction and convince him to modify the means in which he fulfills his charitable giving. The second would be Marty Brewster who could boost the bank account of any club in 30 days!

Next is a man whose recording of Joe Gould's life was so honest that his life became a mirror for the creative tragedy. Joseph Mitchell didn't hold back the truth and, subsequently, was never able to publish again. In contrast, Richard N. Goodwin's pursuit of the truth helped to launch his career in politics while exposing the Twenty One quiz show scandal in 1959.

Like Goodwin, Ben Stein served as a political speech writer and gained national notoriety in the quiz show genre (albeit for the opposing political party and a successful run hosting his own game show). Stein's diverse background and personable demeanor would lend themselves quite well to any community or media outreach a club would need. However, the person that would probably overshadow Stein in this department would be Former First Lady and the First United States Representative to the United Nations Eleanor Roosevelt a woman with numerous talents, countless achievements, and seldom seen charisma.

Now that a former First Lady has been mentioned I am sure you are wondering what presidents I am including in this Rotary club. I have specifically chosen two overlooked presidents rather than repeating the excellent selections that are commonly made. For my list I am including John Tyler (10th President of the United States) and John Quincy Adams (6th President of the United States). Tyler was selected for his assertiveness and his willingness to break with party lines in order to pursue what he thought was the right decision. Whether you agree with him or not (or both) you have to admire someone that insists on pushing forward rather than left or right. Adams' inclusion is because of his long standing impact on the American mentality by authoring what is now known as the Monroe Doctrine and for his dedication to service as he is the only President to serve in the United States House of Representatives after his presidency.

At no other time in modern history has there been so many heroic examples of service above self than those examples that can be found in the testimonies of the Holocaust. From Christian X of Denmark wearing a yellow star and Janusz Korczak refusing to leave his children to Hermine Santruschitz (better known as Miep Gies) helping to hide the Frank family and Oskar Schindler doing whatever they could to save as many lives as they could. All put the lives of others in front of their own in service to humanity.

Many of those who lived through and those who survived that horrific time went on to live lives of a deep and lasting impact to the improvement and healing of the world. While Golda Mier's family had long since left Eastern Europe by the time of the Holocaust, she fought to not only open the gates of the Holy Land but immigration to other countries as well (including the United States) in an attempt to save as many Jews as possible from the Nazi regime.

Fortunately, one man that was able to escape the swift advancement of the Third Reich was Rabbi Menachem Mendel Schneerson (The Lubavitcher Rebbe). His service as a religious leader not only to the Jews but to the world as a whole serves as a model that we are all made in G-d's image. To reinforce this message of peace it is important to have other religious leaders as members of the club to include Karol Józef Wojtyła (Pope John Paul II), Lhamo Dondrub (The 14th Dali Lama), and Mohandas Karamchand Gandhi (Mahatma Ghandi).

Fittingly, the ideal place for this club and this collaboration of religious leaders to meet would be in the Commonwealth of Pennsylvania. To host them would, of course, be William Penn who was an early advocate of democracy and religious freedom. He was also known as someone who maintained good relations and honored treaties with the Lenape Indians.

And to represent the Indians of North America would be two overlooked and powerful men. The first is Jim Thorpe who was a dominant athletic force that, toward the end of his life, he was named the greatest athlete of the first half of the 20th century (above all the greats including Babe Ruth). Since that time, his legacy continues to fade in the mind of the public and his name is all too often forgotten.

The final Rotarian at the table would be Amoroleck, Chief of the Monacan Indian Nation, who was captured by John Smith in September 1608. The Monacan Nation has been largely forgotten by history and can't be found in a common school text book. Because of colonial bias and historical influence on settlers by their rival nation, the Powhatans, the Monacan people have been pushed aside and 'edited out' of the historical record. Maybe by having Chief Amoroleck present, we can revise the text.

So, that is my round table of Rotarians. There are many others that came to mind obviously but this is the mix that I thought would promote the most discussion amongst the members as well as providing some structure and leadership to the club. I did my best to pull together a list of people that don't immediately come to mind (of course, there are always a few exceptions).

Now let's make things interesting… below is a list of alternative members (also mostly of the uncommon variety and all of which could have easily been included above). Would you swap out any of the above with any of the people found below? Are there any other people that the club cannot do without?

King Solomon
Edward VIII
Joshua Lawrence Chamberlain
Chris Kyle
John Moses Browning
Colin L. Powell
Ted Williams
Kevin Smith
James Earl Jones
Helen Keller

Will it be BENEFICIAL
to all concerned?

Important Takeaways From RLI And Other Rotary Events

Induction to Induction: My First Year As A Rotarian

My Rotary experience during my first year (2012-2013) was quite different than most first year Rotarians. By joining a smaller club, I knew that I would be able to have an immediate impact and I would have the opportunity to quickly establish my presence in the club. This isn't always the case as this is reliant upon an open minded membership of trusting and supportive men and women. Fortunately, I am a member of such a club.

Since I joined Rotary in August 2012, I have had a wide range of experiences and I have held numerous offices. I quickly established myself as a board member and almost immediately took upon the role of Sergeant-At-Arms. In early 2013 I gratefully accepted the honor of becoming the Vice President of the club and later that year I was, along with all the other incoming officers, officially inducted as the President Elect of the Rotary Club of Bala Cynwyd – Narberth by Past District Governor Joel Chesney. It was also a great day to have my wife attend her first Rotary meeting with me!

I have done my best to represent the club and Rotary as a whole in a positive light in the community and I look forward to doing so in this new role. I look forward to both supporting our incoming President, Dr. Sherman Leis, as well as bringing ideas and strategies to the table that will both enhance and expand upon the goals established under his leadership. However, these initiatives are dependent upon a strong and engaged membership that is motivated by the ability of Rotary to change lives. Thankfully, we have such a membership.

I have made it known both in person and in writing what my goals are going into this new Rotary year and I am looking forward to seeing all of them to fruition. These and similar goals should be adopted by all service centric clubs as we are all essential to the community especially in this time where technology has widened our world it is important for us to bring people back to center. We must take pride in the community and do all that we can to ensure the success of our neighborhoods, cities, towns, etc.

Our club has a long history in the community having received our charter in 1926 by sponsorship from the Rotary Club of Philadelphia. While the community around us has changed, our presence and commitment has never wavered and we will continue in our duty to remain a grounding constant among our neighbors. As part of the world's oldest and largest community service club of its kind, we will continue to serve as a doorway to a greater world where service is placed above self and the morals set forth by Rotary permeate our daily lives.

I take great pride in many things not the least of which is my Rotary club and I am humbled by the responsibility entrusted in me by my fellow Rotarians. While our club is small, preventing us from changing the ebb and flow of the tide, we can still create waves by making ripples in the water. This is how we make our presence known in the community and impact the world around us. One on one, person to person, we can change lives for the better. What greater meaning can there be in life?

Can We Make This Campaign Obsolete?

For many of us, looking back at old class photos and school portraits is not a pleasant experience and for some can be downright disturbing. Those days were not something that I particularly looked forward to and looking at them now that sentiment is quite evident. The same can be said for many instances during the course of one's life when they sit for a portrait of some form. However, yesterday was not one of those days.

With assistance from the officers, members of The Rotary Club of Bala Cynwyd –Narberth took turns taking photos for "The World's Biggest Commercial" campaign to benefit the PolioPlus program. The basis of the campaign is simple, "the world's largest health initiative deserves the World's Biggest Commercial". Since Rotary International has millions of members around the world this should not just be a possibility, it should be a given.

Since 1985, Rotary's commitment to End Polio Now has resulted in the immunization of more than 2 billion children worldwide against polio decreasing the number of those affected by more than 99 percent (from approximately 350,000 reported cases every year in the beginning to fewer than 700 new cases reported in 2011). Of course, this success would have not been possible without the efforts of Rotarians worldwide as well as the generous partnerships that have been formed over the years including those with the Bill and Melinda Gates Foundation, PhRMA, and many others. We truly are 'This Close'.

What is needed now is for Rotary leaders to motivate their membership and make further contributions to the eradication of this paralyzing disease. Take action and show your support. Go to the website and follow the simple instructions: Snap a photo of yourself making the 'This Close' sign and upload it into the commercial. Show it to your friends and family and ask them to do the same. Your involvement will help convince world leaders that support for polio eradication is global.

How much do you value life? How much do you value the 60 seconds it takes to contribute to this effort? This is truly a once in a lifetime, once in a generation, the one opportunity we have to ensure future generations are lifted of this burden. Our goal is to see that this program becomes obsolete. Help us to close the gap and make polio are part of the past rather than the future.

The Foundation Of Our Work

Saturday was training day. Not the Denzel Washington type rather a day comprised of proper procedures, deadlines, and requirements in order to apply for Rotary Foundation grants. Nine hours later and I am finally able to apply for and utilize funds to help the community. Needless to say, this is a useful and necessary ability for every club and one that I hope to apply in the near future.

However, there was much more to the day than simply information. Much of the time was spent inspiring those in attendance with the accounts of fellow Rotarians who have seen their work come to fruition. From securing medical equipment for a community in desperate need and ensuring that fresh water is available to people who live without running water to founding a new industry in West Africa that allows the people to support themselves with skills taught by committed Rotarians. All of these projects took hard work, dedication, and funds provided, in part, by the Rotary Foundation.

It really is awe inspiring to see the work that has been done and to meet the people that have brought those projects to fruition. It is what keeps me motivated to continue to raise the funds needed for our own educational projects in West Philadelphia. Yesterday in particular it pushed me to sell more tickets for our fundraiser and brainstorm with other clubs about what we might be able to achieve in the near future by working together.

Hearing about the projects, listening to the long time Rotarians in attendance, and learning from the district and international leadership is a means to give us all a common experience. Regardless of the communities we each live in and the focus that each of our clubs may have, we are all Rotarians and we are all taking the steps in our own ways to better the world. We all may have different backgrounds and varying years of Rotary service, from Rotary International Past President Wilf Wilkinson with nearly 50 years to someone like myself with just over a year, we are all equal. We are all contributors to peace in this world.

These kinds of events are an opportunity not just to ensure that we have the proper training but that we are able to discuss with other clubs about the work that we are doing. We are able to find a common ground and in many instances find partners in our endeavors. This is a time to do the behind the scenes work that makes our projects so effective and ensures the longevity and sustainability of our efforts.

These are the types of moments that reinforce my decision to spend a rare day off in a conference room at a Holiday Inn. This is what gets me out of bed at five in the morning and out the door by six. This is why we give so much of our time and energy. Knowing that we are able to accomplish such great things not as individuals but as a part of something greater than ourselves is the reason why we are Rotarians.

Never Settle For Disappointment

My Rotary week started off on a high point as I was looking forward to representing my club on The 4th of July in the parade in Center City Philadelphia. However, that anticipation was soon extinguished as district participation in the parade was cancelled due to not enough people registering for the event. I guess I can add this to my list of goals for next year to rally my club and the clubs in the district to participate. I choose to look forward to next year at this point.

Wednesday quickly rolled around and I was at Aldar Bistro for our regular meeting. I guess you could say that this was both a high point and a low point as I was happy that we had a great meeting and we were able to talk a bit more in depth about the recent transition but the disappointing part was that we were a small group of three. Great company, great discussion, poor turnout; I guess Wednesday could be considered a wash.

Independence Day was a great day, as it is every year, but also in a Rotary sense as well. My wife and I started our day (we slept in quite a bit) by heading into Narberth and selling popcorn at the town carnival to benefit the club. We only signed up for a two hour 'shift' but I really don't know where the time went even with a temperamental popcorn cart. It was a great event that I look forward to repeating next year after the parade.

Later that evening, as I was finishing my daily writing and listening to the sounds of fireworks reverberating off the neighboring apartment building, I received a message from a fellow Rotarian I met at a district event some time ago and with whom I have stayed in touch. He had recently read a piece I wrote about doing the research in order to join the Sons of the American Revolution and wanted to connect me with someone who could help with the genealogy research. This is excellent news not just for me but for my family as we are all looking forward to learning more and taking this final step of solidifying and verifying this research. I am looking forward to exploring all six lines (at present count) further and updating my relatives.

So, overall, it could have been a better week but I am content with the Rotary activity this week. What started with a little disappointment was quickly followed by great fellowship on Wednesday and satisfying service and an unexpected camaraderie on Thursday. I would say that is a pretty good week that I wouldn't mind repeating every week.

Graduation Weekend

While I did miss my usual Rotary club meeting in Bala Cynwyd on Wednesday I was still able to get my Rotary fix on Saturday. Somehow I was able to make myself crawl out of bed at six in the morning, pick up a couple of my fellow Rotarians, and make my way to King of Prussia for the third, and final, installment of my Rotary Leadership Institute (RLI) training. By the end of the day I was a graduate.

Regional events such as this are both a great learning opportunity but also a tremendous social experience as well with people in attendance from a variety of states all there for the same purpose, to become better Rotarians. As always, it was a diverse group of people ranging in age (20's to 80's), occupation/vocation, and Rotary experience (I met people who joined within the past year as well as people who have been proud Rotarians for over 50 years). These aspects were much like my previous takeaways from other sessions and events that I have attended but there was something a little different for me this time around.

It all started during the registration process. As I waited for my information to be retrieved and I was writing the check, I ran into a young man who was a guest speaker at our club earlier in the year. We had gotten together for coffee afterward to talk about Rotary and, at the time, I offered my perspective on the Rotary experience and assisted him in reaching out to other clubs. We hadn't been able to reconnect since but now I was seeing him, a newly minted Rotarian, taking the next step in becoming a leader in his club. Albeit small, I am glad I was able to play a role in his decision to join.

Heading into the first session of the day, I took a look around the room and noticed many familiar faces. There were a handful of us that have attended level two together and now we found ourselves reuniting for round three. While we were all from different clubs, districts, and states we all picked up from where we left off as if we had known one another for years. Needless to say, my comfort level was significantly higher this time around.

With class underway time seemed to fly by with a group of excellent instructors that knew just the right direction to take us and questions to ask. It was at this point that I came to realize just how far I had come as I was able to answer questions and make contributions with certainty rather than with a tentative tone (of course, it didn't hurt that one of the sessions was entirely about PR and communications). This third and final part of the training really was a culmination not just in the educational sense but in shifting my mentality. For the first time I felt as if I was ready to be a leader within Rotary.

I am positive that I would have come to this actualization without RLI but I have no idea how long it would have taken and whether or not I could be as effective of a leader without it. In general, with the past couple of years being so tumultuous, I am glad that I have had the consistency and guidance that Rotary and my fellow Rotarians have offered to me. While our goal as Rotarians is to serve others and our communities we can't deny the service that Rotary has offered to each and every one of us in making us better people.

Now the question remains, do I move forward and attend graduate classes or should I give back and become an instructor or both? I guess we will just have to wait and see.

About The Author

Sean M. Teaford was inducted into The Rotary Club of Bala Cynwyd – Narberth in August of 2012 and quickly assumed a leadership role in the club serving as Sargent-At-Arms, Vice President, and President Elect in rapid succession. Sean started numerous initiatives at the club level, has been a speaker at various district events, and is also a graduate of the Rotary Leadership Institute (RLI). While no longer an active Rotarian, he remains loyal to the lessons learned and leadership skills acquired while an officer with the club.

In addition to his community service efforts, over the past fifteen years, Sean has gained a reputation as a talented poet and insightful essayist with honest images that remain with the reader long after the page has been turned. He has published hundreds of poems, over a thousand print and online articles, and has authored seven collections of poetry and essays while currently maintaining a daily blog, Time To Keep It Simple, which has served as a record of his life as a traveler, writer, genealogist, photographer, Rotarian, Mason, convert to Judaism, husband, and new father.

Sean received his M.F.A. in Creative Writing from Rosemont College and B.A. in English from Endicott College. In addition to serving as an editor for a variety of literary publications, including *The Endicott Review* and *The Mad Poets Review*, he has coordinated numerous poetry readings and programs across the Northeast and has been a featured speaker in the Boston and Philadelphia areas.

A public relations account executive, Sean lives in Morgantown, Pennsylvania with his wife and young son.

Printed in the United States
By Bookmasters